PIANO/VOCAL/GUITAR

JUSTINTIMBERLAKE
FUTURESEX/LOVESOUNDS

ISBN-13: 978-1-4234-2337-9
ISBN-10: 1-4234-2337-2

HAL•LEONARD®
CORPORATION
7777 W. BLUEMOUND RD. P.O. BOX 13819 MILWAUKEE, WI 53213

Visit Hal Leonard Online at
www.halleonard.com

FUTURESEX/LOVESOUND

Words and Music by JUSTIN TIMBERLAKE,
TIM MOSLEY and NATE HILLS

See, ev-'ry-bod-y says you're hot, ba - by,

but can you make it hot for me?

Said, if you're think-ing 'bout hold-ing back, don't wor - ry, girl, ___

'cause I'm gon-na make it so eas - y.

So slide a lit-tle bit clos-er to me, lit-tle girl.

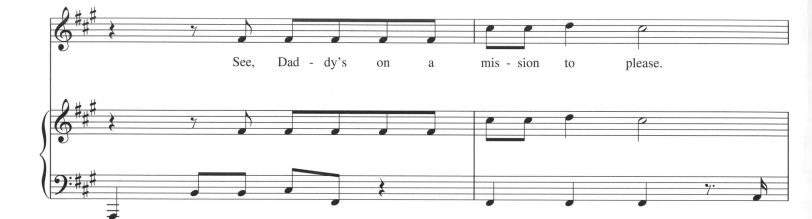

See, Dad-dy's on a mis-sion to please.

Wait a sec-ond. She's hopped up on me.

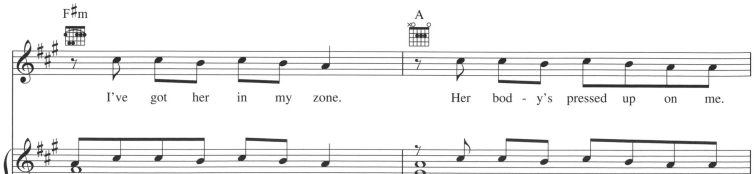

I've got her in my zone. Her bod-y's pressed up on me.

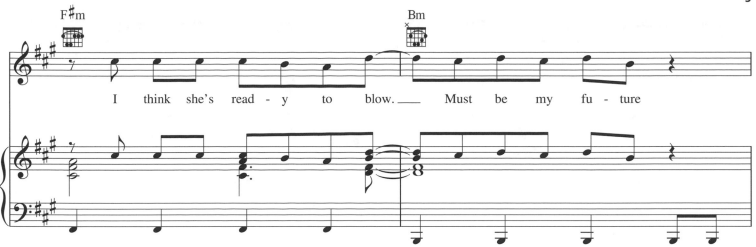

I think she's read-y to blow. ___ Must be my fu - ture

sex love sound. And when it goes down,

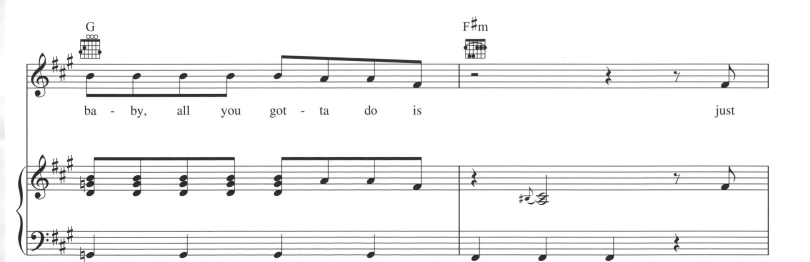

ba - by, all you got - ta do is just

tell me which way you like ___ that. All you got - ta do is

And your en - e - my __ are your thoughts, ba - by,

so just let 'em go. _____

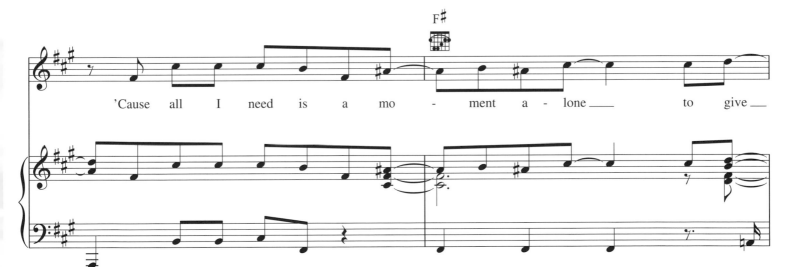

F#

'Cause all I need is a mo - ment a - lone __ to give __

Bm   F#

__ you my tone __ and get you out of con - trol.

Must be my fu - ture sex love sound.

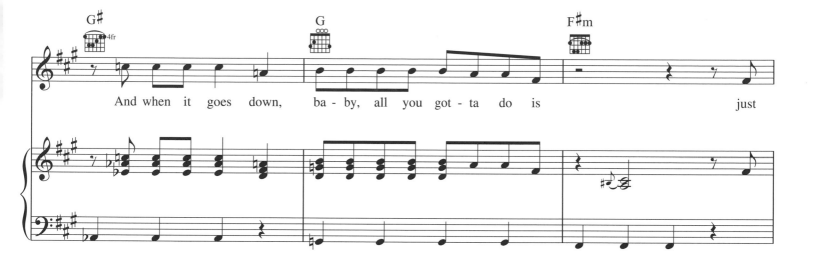

And when it goes down, ba - by, all you got - ta do is just

tell me which way you like ___ that. All you got - ta do is

tell me which way you like ___ that. Do you like it like this? Do you like it like that?

Tell me which way you like ___ that. Uh - huh, ___ huh, huh, oh.

Tell me which way you like ___ that.

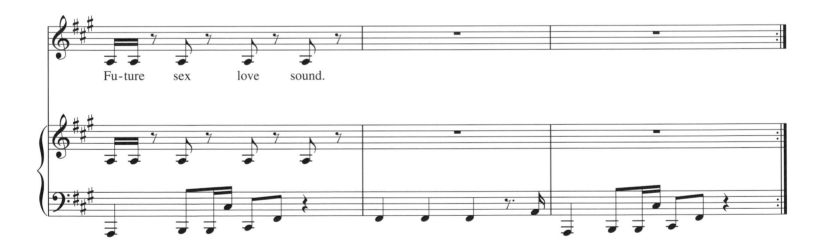

Fu - ture sex love sound.

Fu - ture sex love sound.

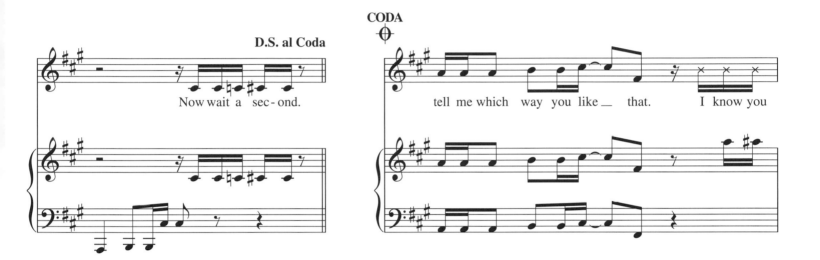

D.S. al Coda

CODA

Now wait a sec - ond.

tell me which way you like __ that. I know you

like it like that.

Tell me which way you like __ that.

Uh - huh, __ huh, huh, oh. Tell me which way you like __ that.

SEXYBACK

Words and Music by JUSTIN TIMBERLAKE,
TIM MOSLEY and NATE HILLS

D.S. al Coda

that's a fact. (Yea!) Take 'em to the cho - rus.

CODA

N.C. Get your sex - y on. Ooh, ooh,

ooh, you rea - dy, yes. Ooh, ooh,

ooh, you rea - dy, yes. Ooh, ooh, ooh, yes.

Ooh, ooh, ooh, ahh, __ ooh.

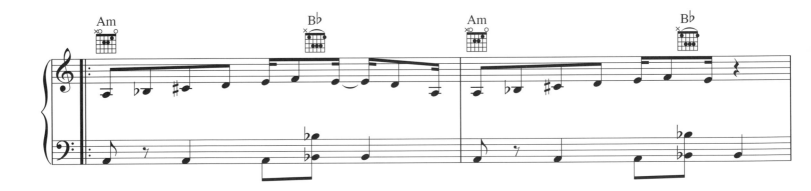

Repeat and Fade | **Optional Ending**

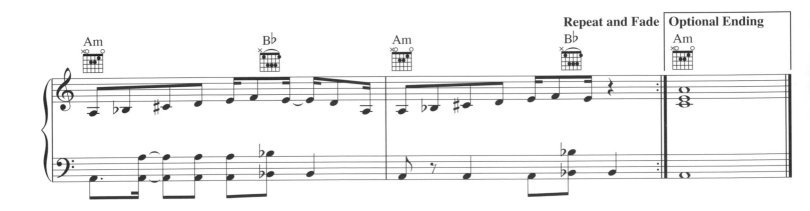

SEXY LADIES
Let Me Talk to You (Prelude)

Words and Music by JUSTIN TIMBERLAKE,
TIM MOSLEY and NATE HILLS

I can tell you want a drink, girl, you ain't got-ta wor-ry no more. _
girl-y from up - town who's wait-in' just to ca-ter to me. _

They keep my bot-tles cold and they pop 'em as soon as I walk in the door. _
I know a lit-tle Bet-ty from down-town that'll do an-y-thing that I please. _

These dudes _ don't know me from Ad-am and Eve, that's why they can't mess up my flow. _
All, _ my p-peo-ple, they dance _ 'round _ when they hear me rock-in' the groove. _

Recorded a half step lower.

And when this beat drops, your heart stops, you feel it from your head to your toes.
Now it might sound cock-y, but is it real-ly cock-y if you know that it's true?

If you know what I'm talk - in' 'bout, (Hey girl) let me see you

work it out. (Hey girl) Girl, that's what I'm talk - in' 'bout. *(Spoken:) Yo Justin, talk to 'em.*

I've got sex-y la - dies (Oh, ooh) all o - ver the floor. You're

talk - in' to one of the great - est (Oh, _____ oh) who did it be - fore. _ Now I'm

back with one of my lat - est. (Oh, _____ ooh) _ Just let - ting you know _ that

I've got sex - y la - dies, so back up some more _ and

1
let me take it off. I know a lit - tle let me take it off.

2
(Sex - y,

sex - y, sex - y, walk that bod - y, talk that bod - y. Sex - y,

sex - y, sex - y, walk that bod - y, talk that bod - y.) (Sex - y,

talk that bod - y.) Yeah, now break it down.

(Spoken:) Now move a little bit to the left.   *Now move back over here to the*

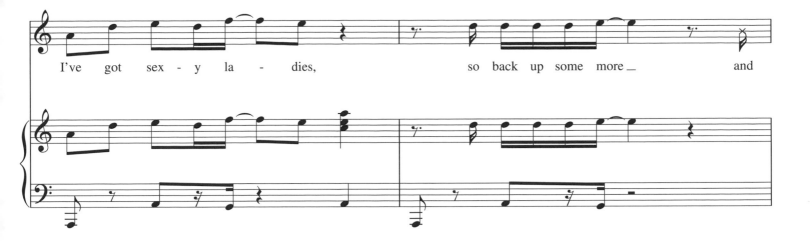

I've got sex - y la - dies, so back up some more ___ and

let me take it off.

Play 3 times

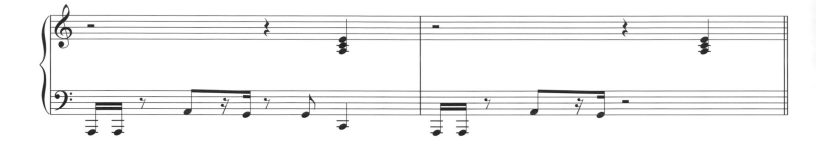

Play 3 times

Moderately fast

N.C.

Play 3 times

(My

Play 6 times

love,   my   love,   my   love,   my   love,   my

love,   my   love,   my   love.)   Rap I: *(See rap lyrics)*

(My love, my love, my love, my love, my love, my love.)

Play 3 times

Rap Lyrics

Rap I: I love the way you standin'.
Lips look so sweet, like cotton candy.
That don't mean you gotta stop dancin',
'Cause the way that you move is so demandin'.
Let's put it on cruise control.
Let me take you to the crib, let me ease your soul.
I'm gonna take it nice and slow,
But first, let me, let me, let me talk to her.

Rap II: Walk into my great place, cozy,
I'm glad you came. Let's make a toast to...
Let me make an indecent proposal,
Let me take you to the back and do what we supposed to.
Let's take a trip to Dubai.
You can be the investigator, I'm your private eye.
You know I want a piece of that pie,
But first, let me, let me, let me talk to her.

MY LOVE

Words and Music by JUSTIN TIMBERLAKE,
TIM MOSLEY, NATE HILLS and CLIFFORD HARRIS

Moderately

Ain't an-oth-er wom-an that could take your spot my...

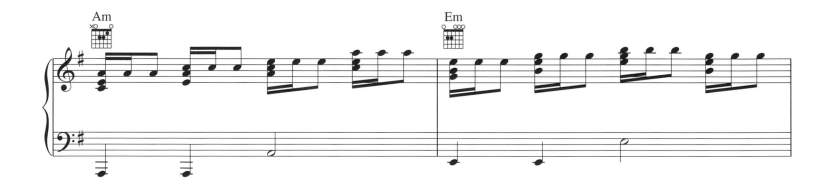

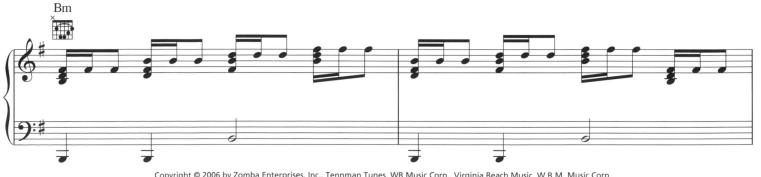

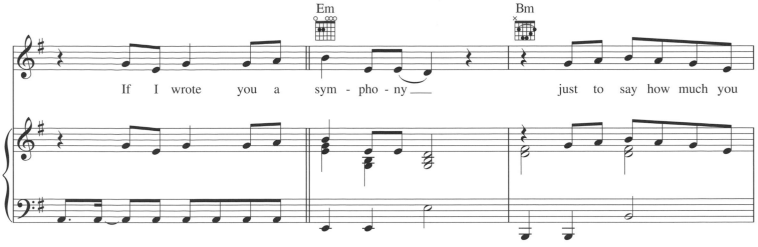

If I wrote you a sym - pho - ny _____ just to say how much you

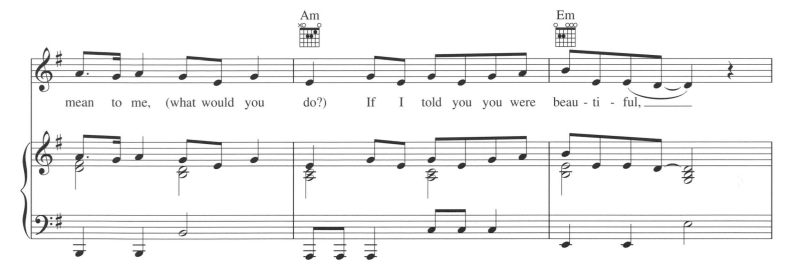

mean to me, (what would you do?) If I told you you were beau - ti - ful, _____

would you date me on the reg - u - lar? (Tell me, would you?) Well, ba - by, I've been a -

round the world, _____ but I ain't seen my - self an - oth - er girl (like

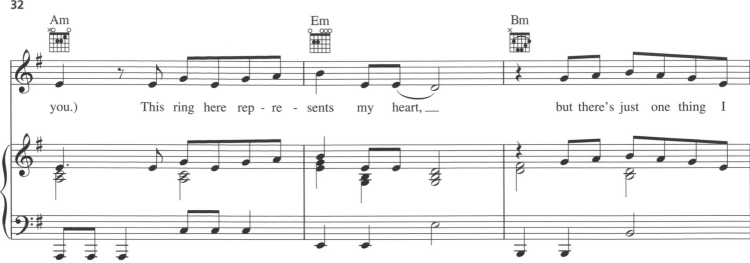

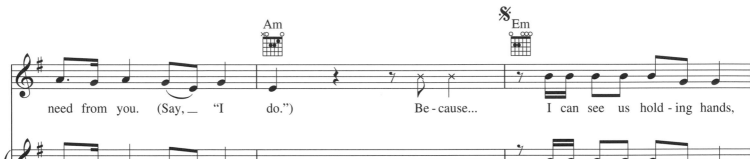

you.) This ring here rep-re-sents my heart, ___ but there's just one thing I

need from you. (Say, ___ "I do.") Be-cause... I can see us hold-ing hands,

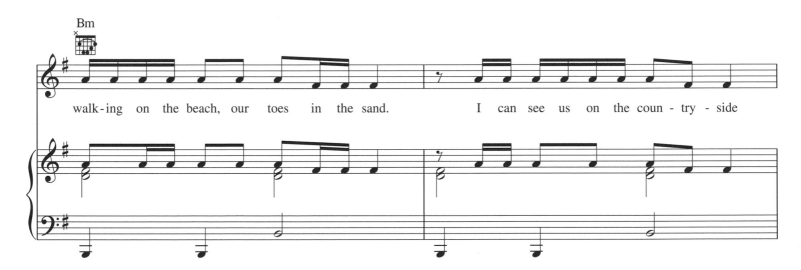

walk-ing on the beach, our toes in the sand. I can see us on the coun-try-side

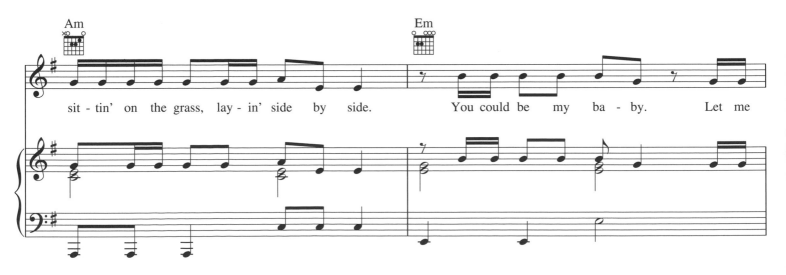

sit-tin' on the grass, lay-in' side by side. You could be my ba-by. Let me

make you my la - dy. Girl, you a - maze me. Ain't got - ta do noth - ing cra - zy. See,

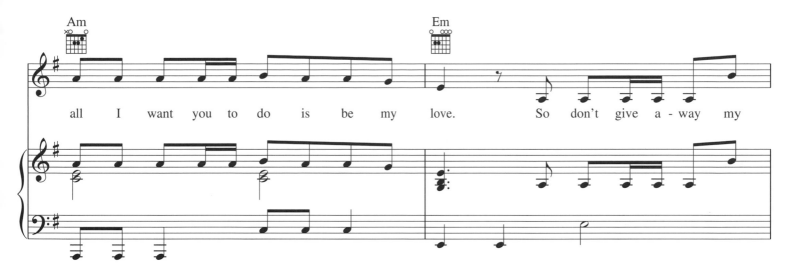

all I want you to do is be my love. So don't give a - way my

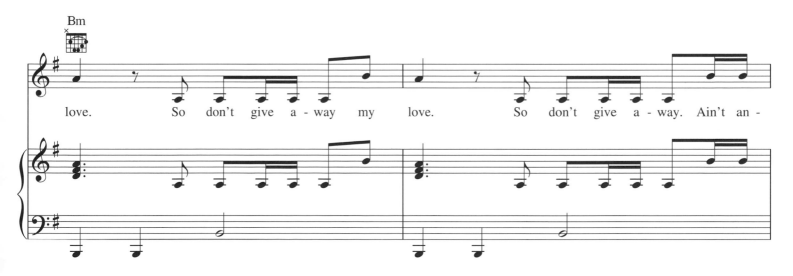

love. So don't give a - way my love. So don't give a - way. Ain't an -

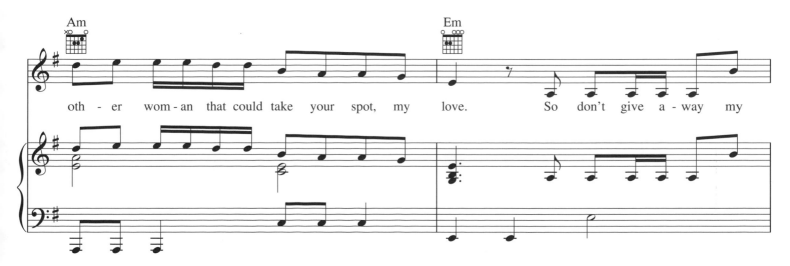

oth - er wom - an that could take your spot, my love. So don't give a - way my

love. So don't give a-way my love. So don't give a-way. Ain't an-

oth - er wom-an that could take your spot, my love, _____

_____ love. _____ My

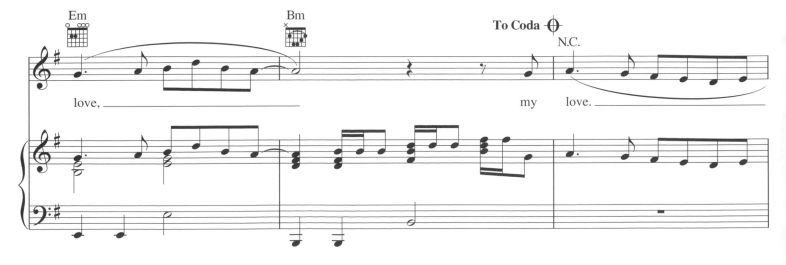

love, _____ my love. _____

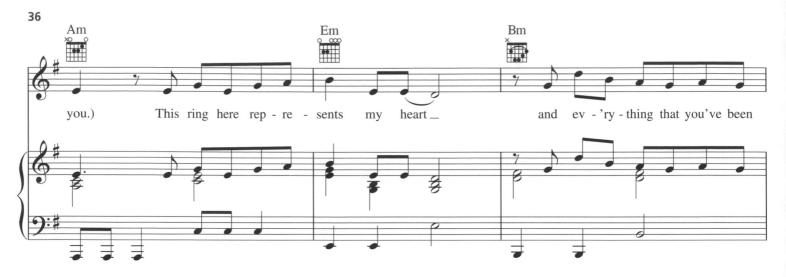

you.) This ring here rep-re-sents my heart __ and ev-'ry-thing that you've been

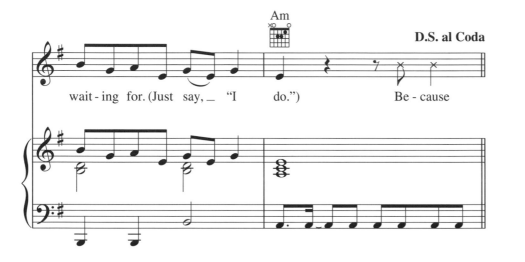

D.S. al Coda

wait-ing for.(Just say, __ "I do.") Be-cause

CODA

love. __
Rap: *(See additional lyrics)*

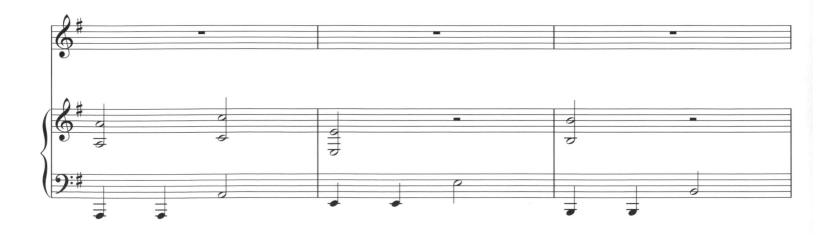

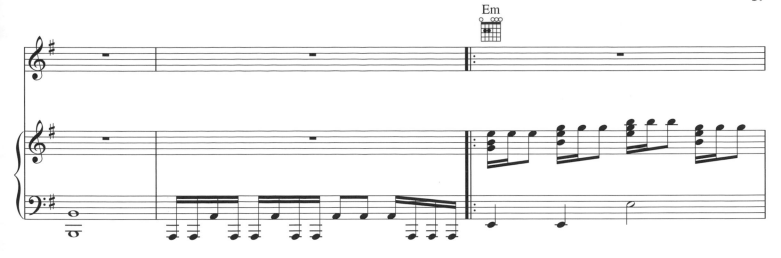

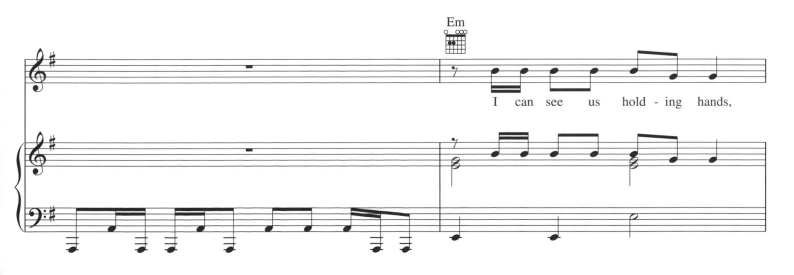

I can see us hold-ing hands,

walk-ing on the beach, our toes in the sand. I can see us on the coun-try-side

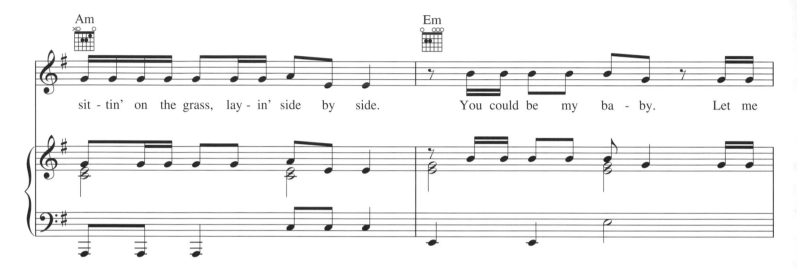

sit-tin' on the grass, lay-in' side by side. You could be my ba-by. Let me

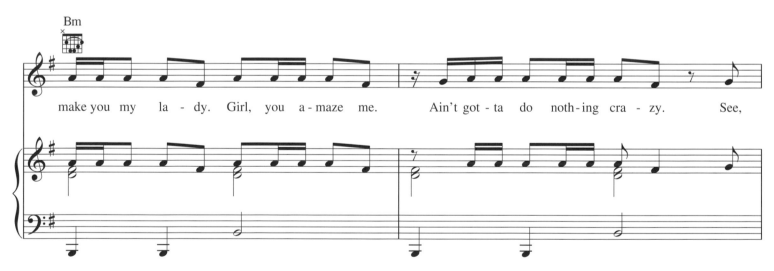

make you my la-dy. Girl, you a-maze me. Ain't got-ta do noth-ing cra-zy. See,

all I want you to do is be my love, love._ My love, love._ My

love, love. ___ Ain't an - oth - er wom - an that could take your spot my

love, ___ love. ___ My

love, ___ my love. ___

Additional Lyrics

Rap: Alright, it's time to get it J.T. I don't know what she hesitating for, man.
   Hey – Shorty cool as a fan and I knew once again and he still has fans from Peru to Japan.
   Hey, listen baby, I don't wanna ruin your plan (naw) but if you got a man, try to lose him if you can.
   'Cause the girl's real wild, throw your hands up high when you wanna come and kick it with a stand-up guy.
   Trust me, you don't really wanna let the chance go by 'cause you ain't been seen with a man so fly.
   Hey baby, friends so fly. I can go fly private 'cause I handle my B-I.
   They call me candle guy. (Why?) Simply 'cause I am on fire. I hate to have to cancel my vacation.
   So you can't deny I'm patient but I ain't gonna try, naw. You don't come, I ain't gonna die.
   Hold up, what you mean you can't go – why? Me and your boyfriend, we ain't no tie.
   You say you wanna kick it when I ain't so high. Well, baby, it's obvious that I ain't your guy.
   I ain't gonna lie, I feel your space, but forget your face. I swear I will.
   St. Barts, Anguilla, anywhere I chill. Just bring with me a pair I will.

LOVESTONED
I Think She Knows (Interlude)

Words and Music by JUSTIN TIMBERLAKE,
TIM MOSLEY and NATE HILLS

Moderately fast

She's freak-y, and she knows it.

She's freak-y, but I like it.

Lis-ten.   She grabs the yel-low bot-tle;   she
shuts the room ___ down, ___ the

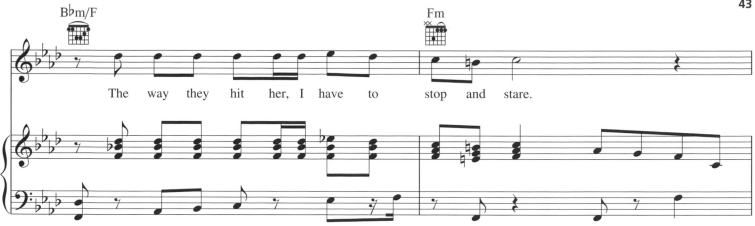

The way they hit her, I have to stop and stare.

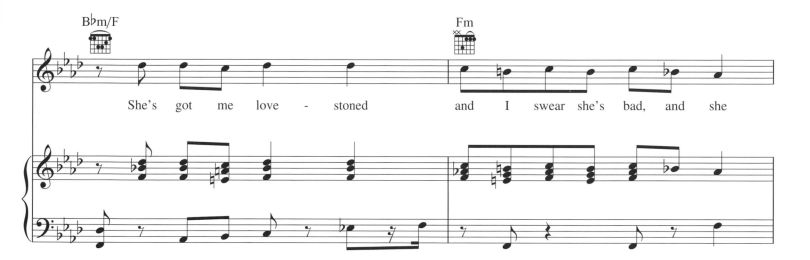

She's got me love - stoned and I swear she's bad, and she

knows, I think that she knows.

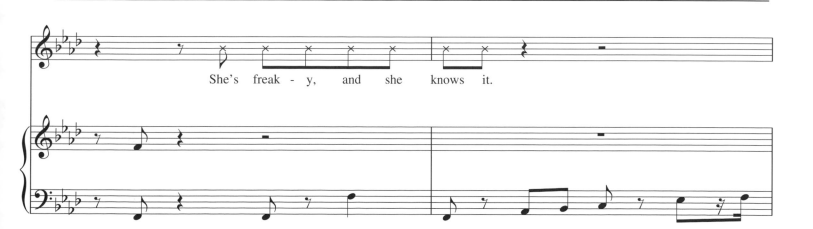

She's freak - y, and she knows it.

She's freak-y, but I like it. Yeah. _

She knows. I think that she

knows. Those flash-in' lights seem to

cause a glare. The way they hit her, I have to

stop and stare. She's got me love - stoned from

ev - 'ry - where. She's bad, and she knows. I think that she

knows. Now dance. Get it,

girl. You're freak - y, but I

stop and stare.   She's got me love - stoned

and I swear she's bad, and she knows.   I think that she

knows.   Those flash - in' lights   seem to   cause a glare.

The way they hit her, I have to   stop and stare.

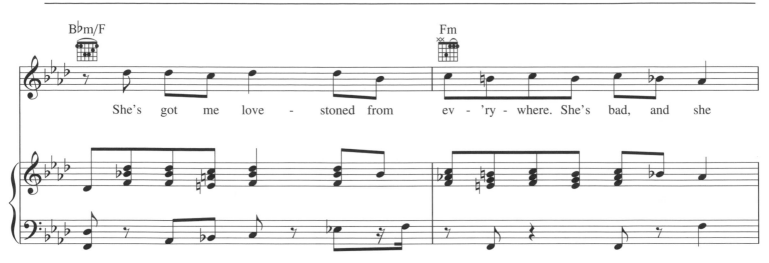

She's got me love - stoned from ev - 'ry - where. She's bad, and she

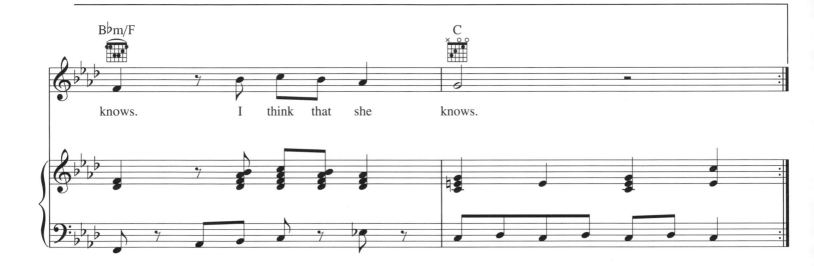

knows. I think that she knows.

knows.

Play 3 times

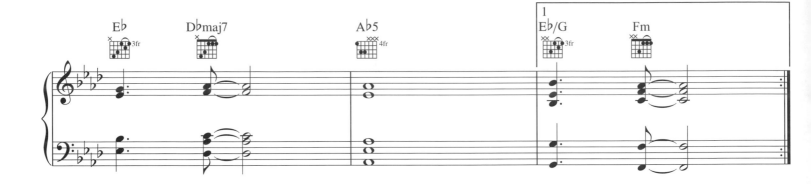

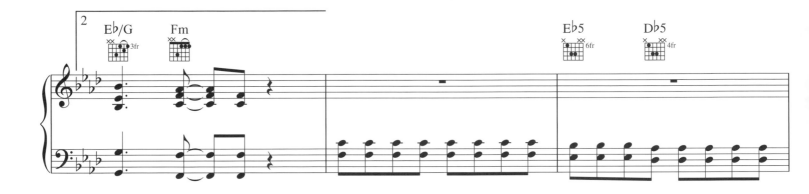

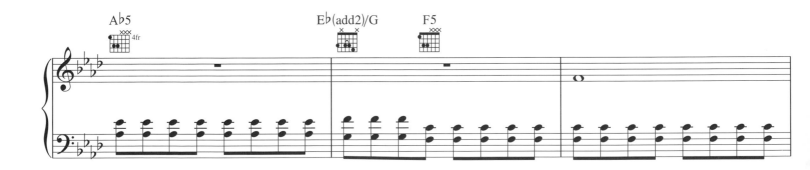

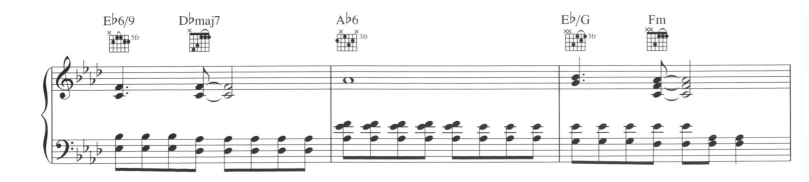

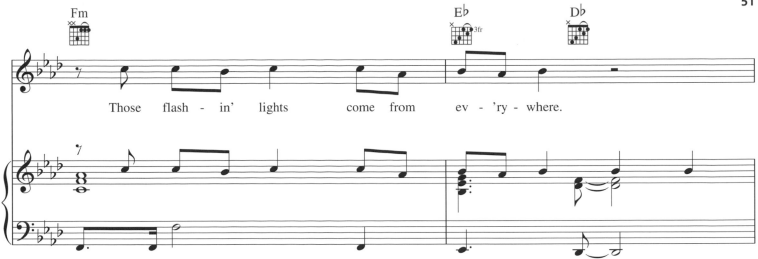

Those flash - in' lights come from ev - 'ry - where.

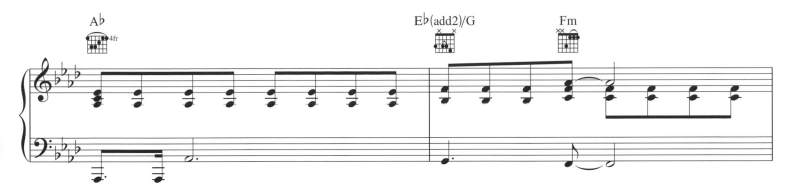

The way they hit her, I just stop and stare.

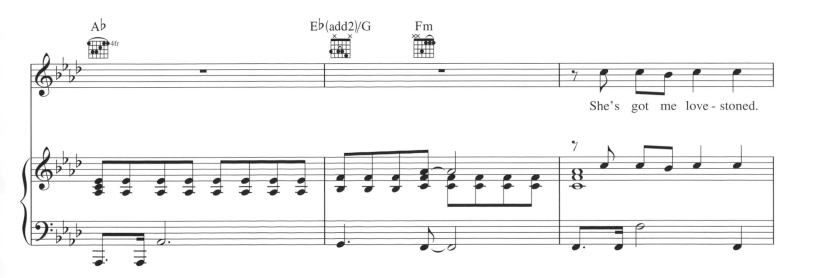

She's got me love - stoned.

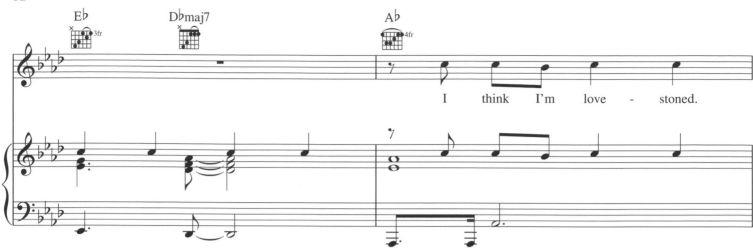

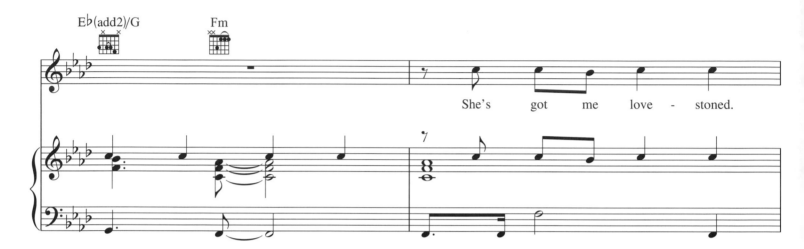

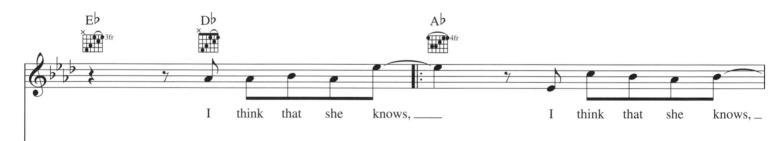

I think that she knows, ___ I think that she knows, __

___ oh, ___ oh. _____ Those flash - in' lights come from

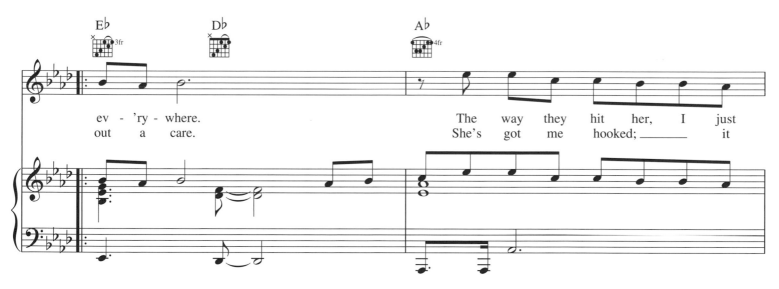

ev - 'ry - where.
out a care.
The way they hit her, I just
She's got me hooked; _____ it

stop and stare. _____ I'm love - stoned from
just ain't fair, but I, _____ I'm love - stoned, and

ev - 'ry - where, and she knows. ___
I could swear that she knows. ___ } I think that she knows, __

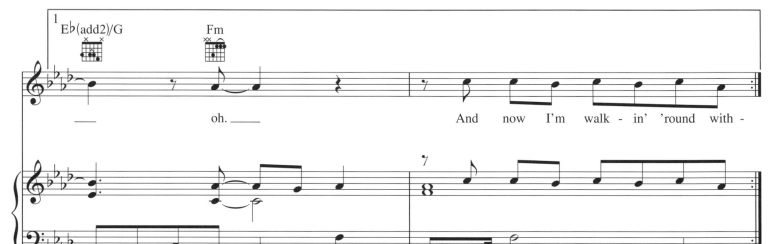

___ oh. ___ And now I'm walk - in' 'round with -

___ oh, ___ oh. ___ She knows, __

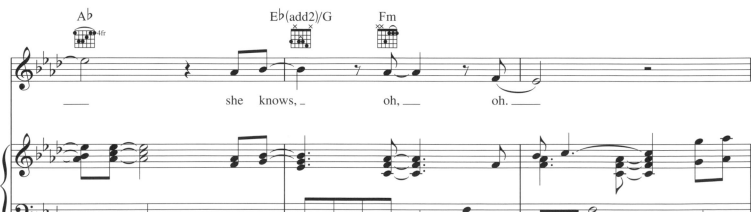

___ she knows, _ oh, ___ oh. ___

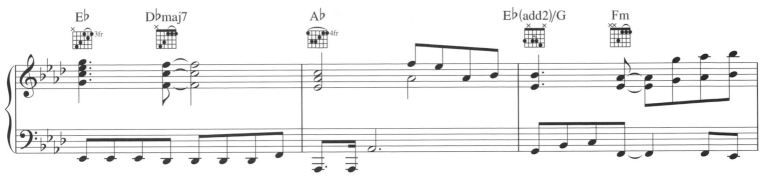

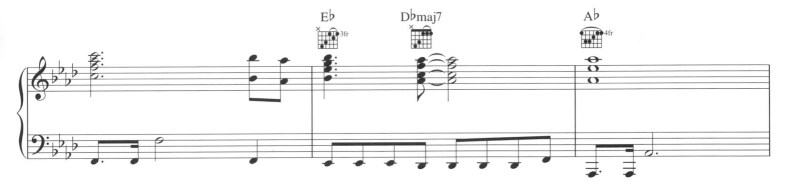

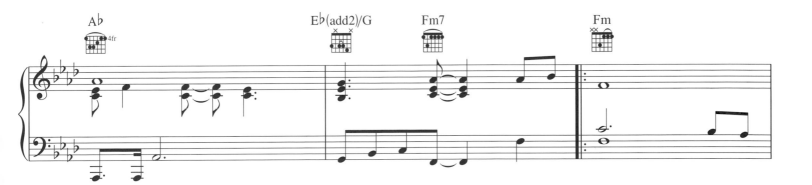

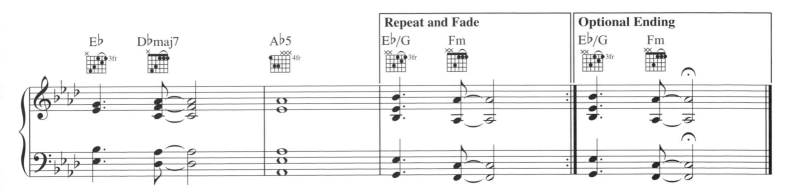

WHAT GOES AROUND
...Comes Around (Interlude)

Words and Music by JUSTIN TIMBERLAKE,
TIM MOSLEY and NATE HILLS

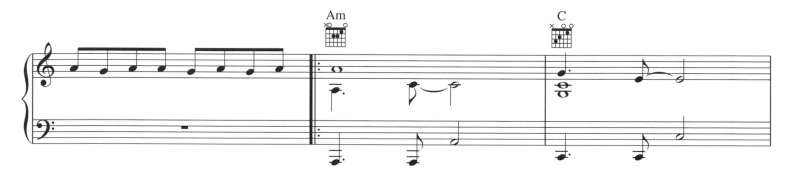

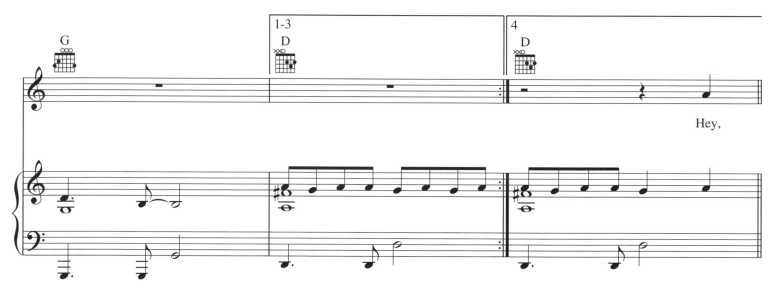

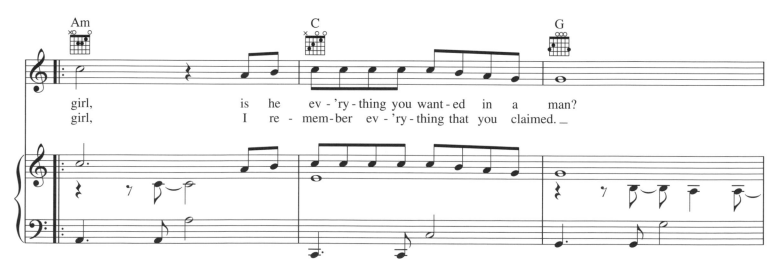

girl, is he ev-'ry-thing you want-ed in a man?
girl, I re-mem-ber ev-'ry-thing that you claimed.

ba - by,   me and you un - til ___ the end, ___ but I guess I was wrong. __

ba - by,   and now ___ it's all just a shame, __ and I guess I was wrong. __

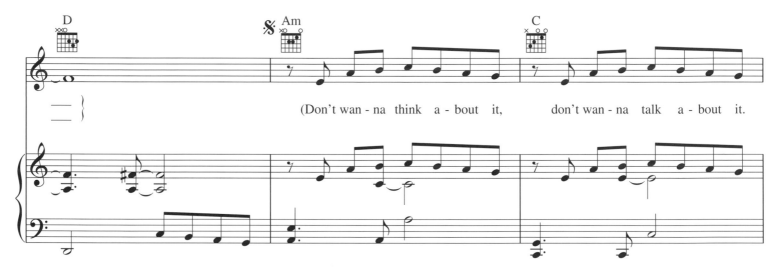

(Don't wan - na think a - bout it,   don't wan - na talk a - bout it.

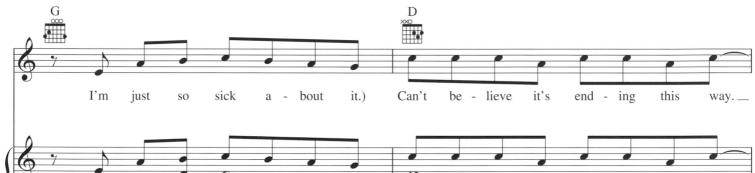

I'm just so sick a - bout it.) Can't be - lieve it's end - ing this way. __

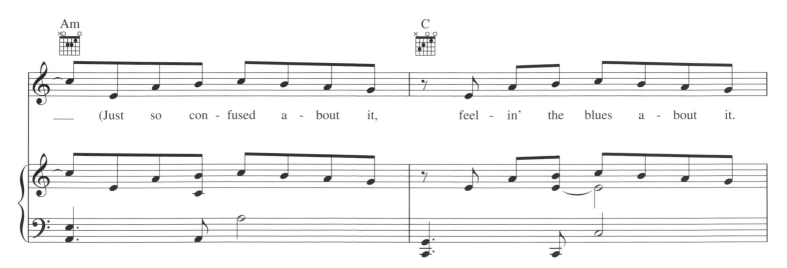

__ (Just so con - fused a - bout it,   feel - in' the blues a - bout it.

break-ing my heart _ to watch you run a-round) 'cause I know that you're liv-ing a lie. _

(But that's o-kay, ba - by, 'cause in time you will _

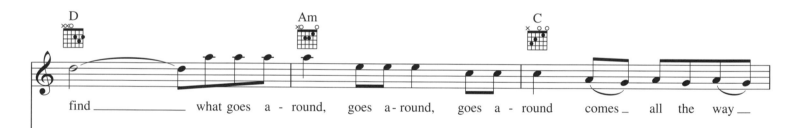

find _____ what goes a-round, goes a-round, goes a-round comes _ all the way _

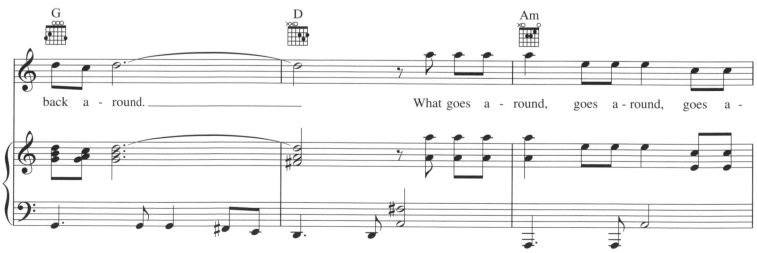

back a-round. _____ What goes a-round, goes a-round, goes a-

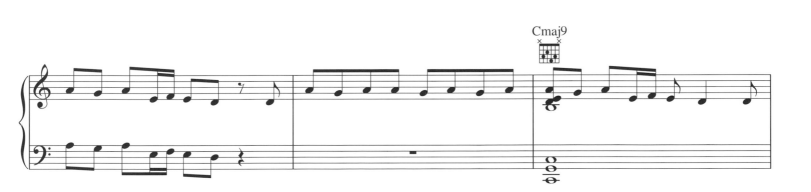

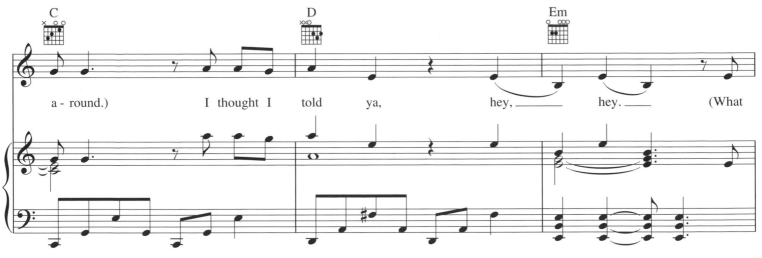

a - round.) I thought I told ya, hey,_____ hey._____ (What

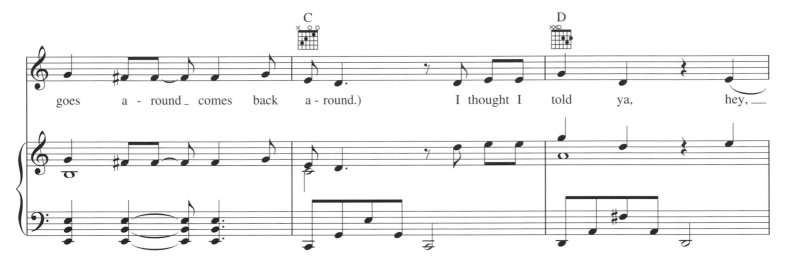

goes a - round__ comes back a - round.) I thought I told ya, hey,___

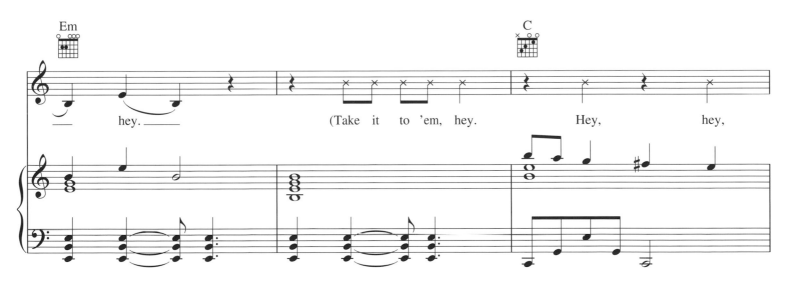

___ hey.___ (Take it to 'em, hey. Hey, hey,

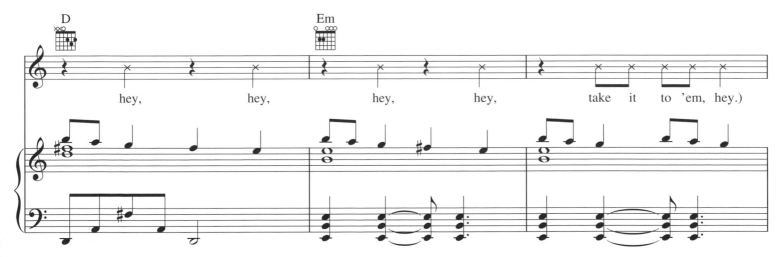

hey, hey, hey, hey, take it to 'em, hey.)

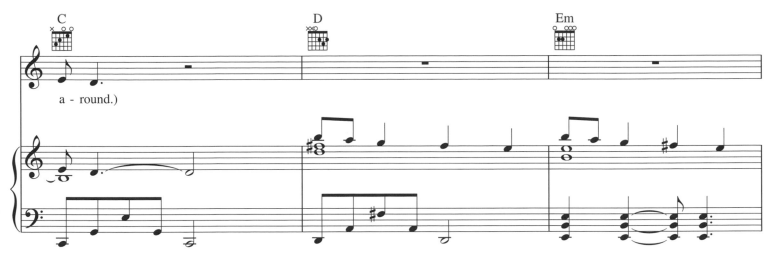

a - round.)

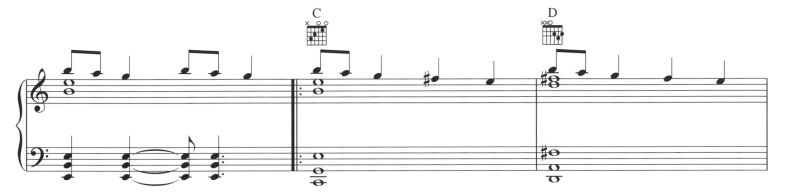

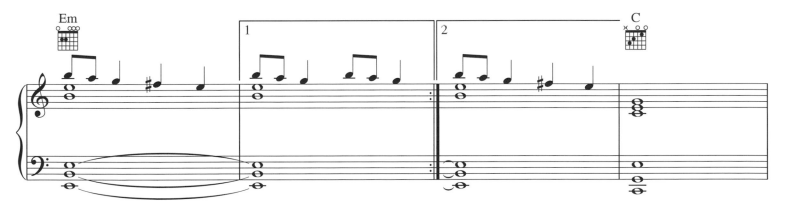

CHOP ME UP

Words and Music by JUSTIN TIMBERLAKE,
TIM MOSLEY and NATE HILLS

* *Recorded a half step lower.*

shape you got up on that frame. I like the way you talk your game. We
I'm ___ just the guest ___ list. ___ I think I need some Ty - le -

might be one and the same. ___ Now I know you got a
nol; you got me rest - less. ___ So grab your friends and let's ___

buzz off that al - co - hol. I got a house that could
take it back to my ___ hive. Let's watch "Sex In The Cit -

en - ter - tain all of y'all. May - be lat - er on
y" or "Des - p'rate House - wives." Si - mon says, ___ "Touch

I'll give you a phone call.
yours ___ while you touch mine."

(Spoken:) Parental discretion

I'm 'bout to slide out, but

Am

I'll get back at ya.
is advised.

And when I call,
Y'all can be the star

don't give me the run-a-round.
in my freak-y spot-light.

I ain't gon' have you try-in' to
Stu-di-o fif-ty-four, ___

play me like a sil-ly clown.
if we get the props ___ right.

Don't sec-ond guess it, girl, there
All we need right now is a

ain't noth - in' to think a - bout,   'cause you got me feind - in', but girl,___
lit - tle bit, a lit - tle bit of act ___ right.   Y'all _ look - in' shy, ___ but y'all

Em

___ you don't hear me.   Lit - tle la - dy (la -
act like y'all don't hear me.

dy, la - dy), you got me just (screwed up)   off ___

___ of your mel - o - dy.   Lit - tle la - dy (la - dy, la - dy), c'mon and don't

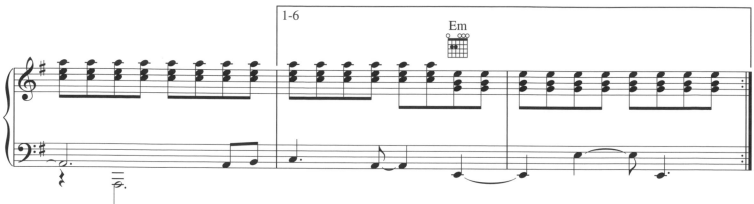

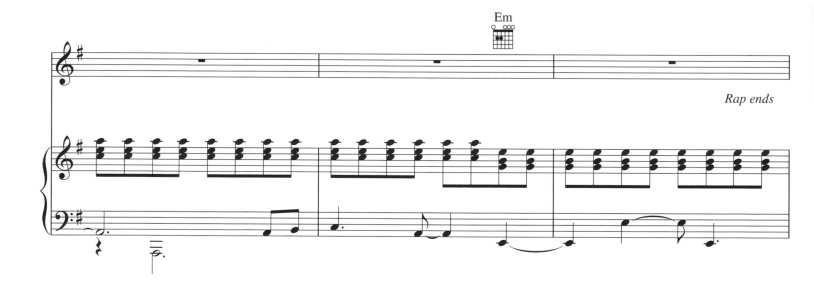

Rap ends

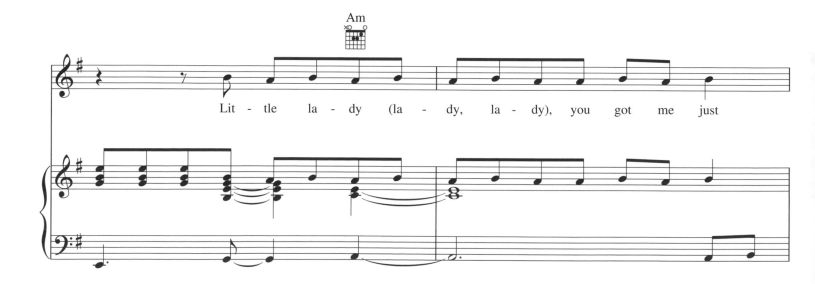

Lit - tle la - dy (la - dy, la - dy), you got me just

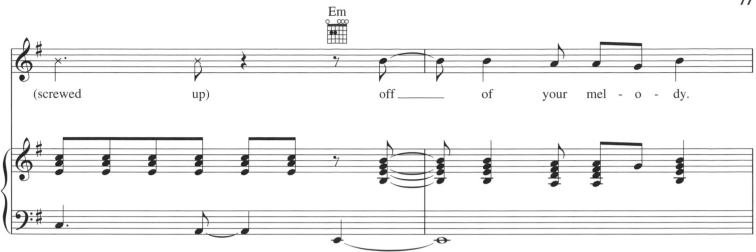

(screwed up) off _____ of your mel - o - dy.

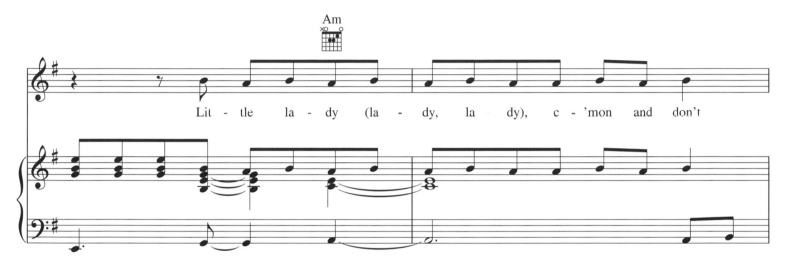

Lit - tle la - dy (la - dy, la - dy), c - 'mon and don't

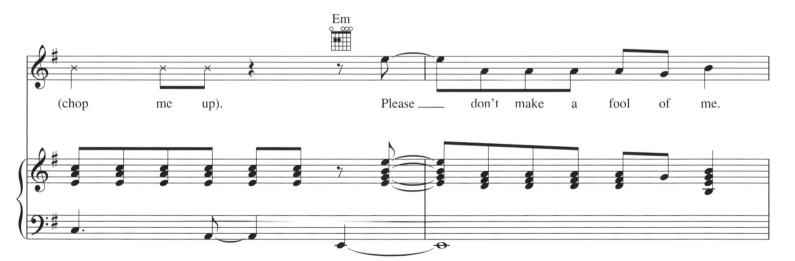

(chop me up). Please _____ don't make a fool of me.

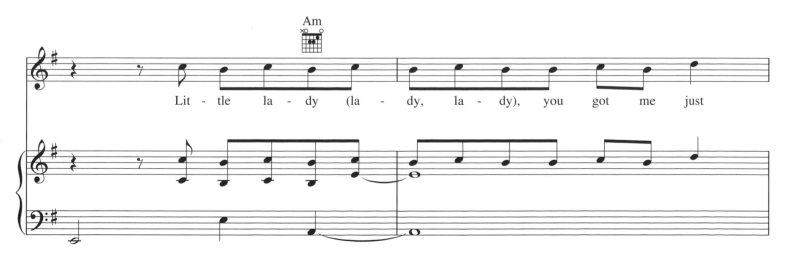

Lit - tle la - dy (la - dy, la - dy), you got me just

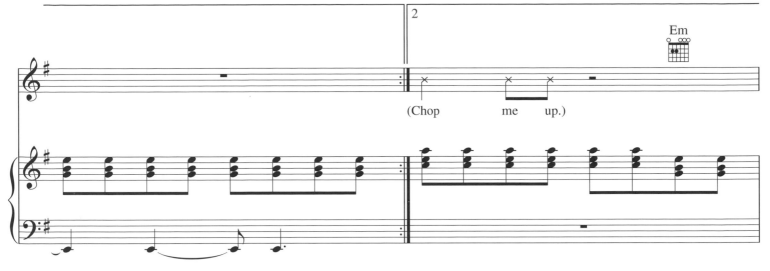

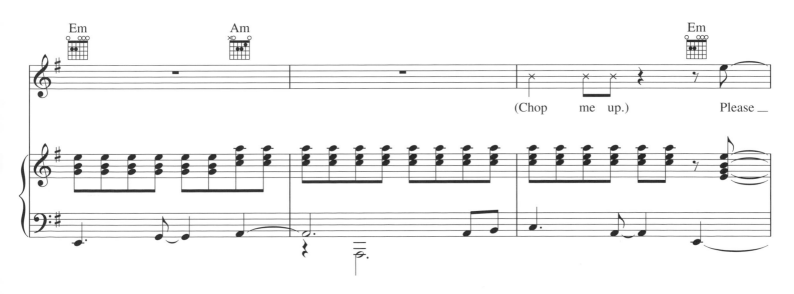

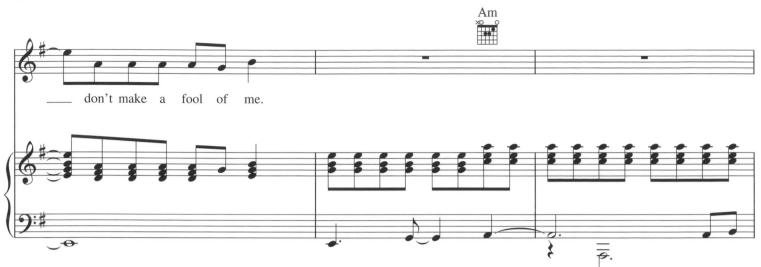

don't make a fool of me.

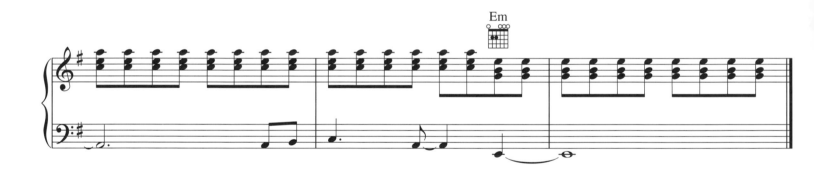

Rap Lyrics

See, girl, you stronger than the strongest drug I ever had.
You could mix them all together; you'd still be twice as bad,
'Cause you're the worst best girlfriend I ever had.
Harder to kick than cigarettes and green bags,
Harder to escape than jail cells and bills mailed.
You had me locked since a bitty girl with pigtails.
Like Michael Jackson, (Why you do me this way?)
Got me cryin' rivers like Timbaland and Timberlake, yeah.
They call me Juicy J, straight up out the Three-6 Mafia.
Ghetto fab player, all these freaks and I'm tryin' to holla at ya.
Quit playin' games, girl, you got my head spinnin' 'round.
I ain't gonna chirp your mobile phone and chase you all over town.
I just want to pick you up and take you to a wrestling match then
(So is it good, is it good) and have a little smack fest.
So if you never call me, I'll be somewhere down in Tennessee,
Washin' away my sorrows in a cold cup of Hennessy.

DAMN GIRL

Words and Music by JUSTIN TIMBERLAKE,
WILL ADAMS, JOSH DAVIS and J.C. DAVIS

Moderately fast

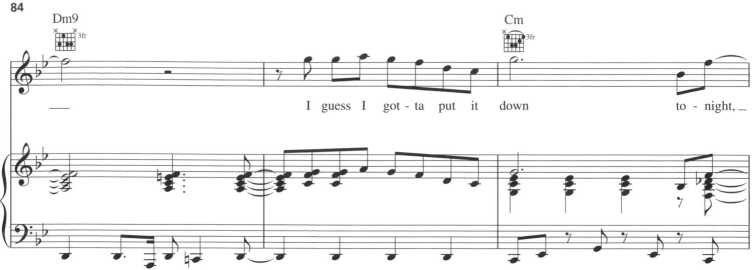

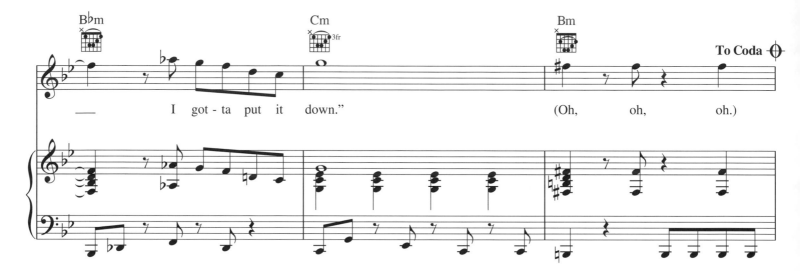

girl, damn, girl, damn. I said there's

some - thin' 'bout the way you do the things you do when you

do the things you do that's got me. (Oh, oh. oh.) I said there's

some - thin' 'bout the way you do the things you do when you

do the things you do that's got me. (Oh, oh, oh.) I said you

CODA

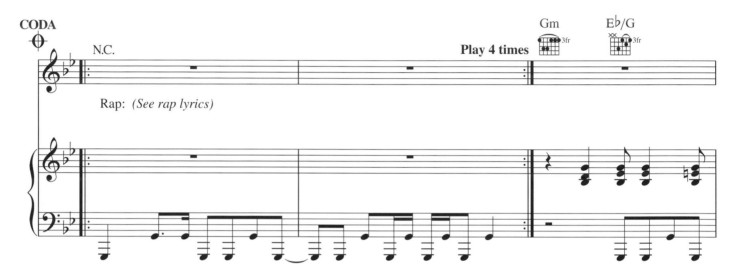

Rap: *(See rap lyrics)*

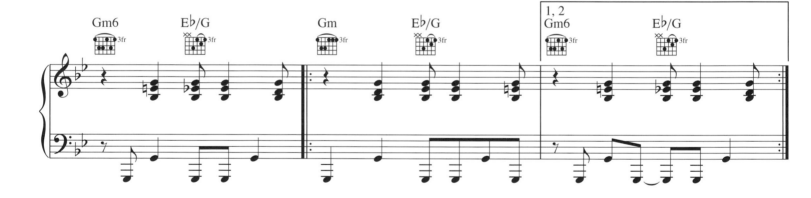

You got me say - in', "Damn, girl,

Rap ends

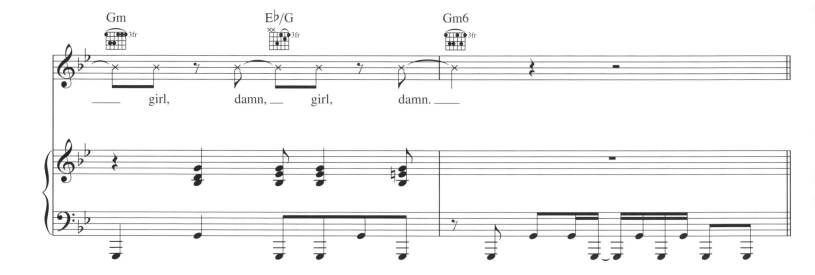

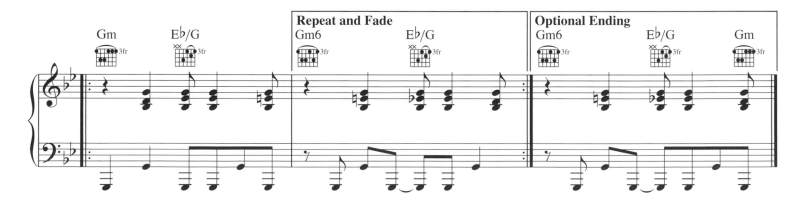

Rap Lyrics

Woo, woo, woo, woo, woo, woo, woo, woo, woo, woo baby.
Give me some of your tasty cinnamon.
Givin' your feminine gelatin,
'Cause got a cinnamon goin' crazy.
Hey, b-b-b-b-b-b-b-baby,
Baby, you're the one I been feindin' for.
When I'm dreamin', I'm dreamin' of you.
When you're gone, I'll be screamin' for you.

So why don't you be my chick and stuff?
Take you out to dinner and catch a flick and stuff.
If we spend time I never get enough.
Girl, you're so fine, make a dark brother blush.
Got me lookin' like a black grape and stuff.
First time I seen you, you had me on crush.
And if you ever give it to me, give it to me rough.
You got me sayin', got me sayin', "Damn."

SUMMER LOVE
Set the Mood (Prelude)

Words and Music by JUSTIN TIMBERLAKE,
TIM MOSLEY and NATE HILLS

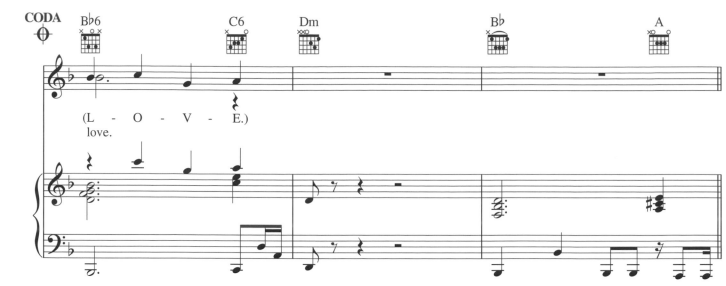

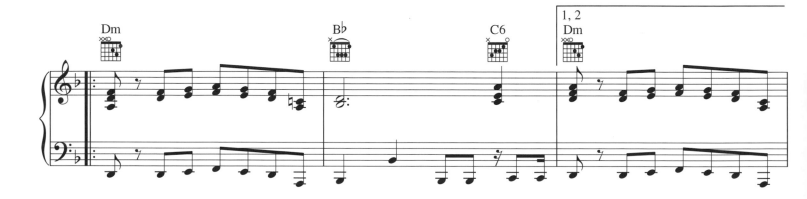

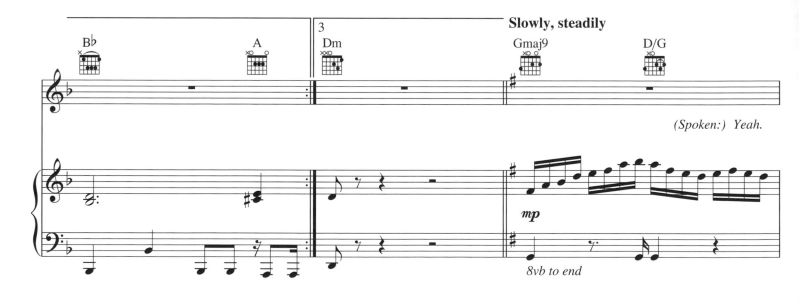

feel all right. _
good to - night. _

Just let me set the

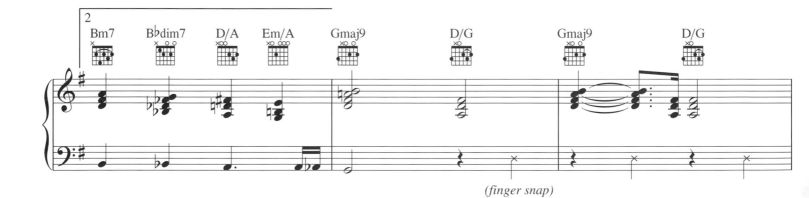

(finger snap)

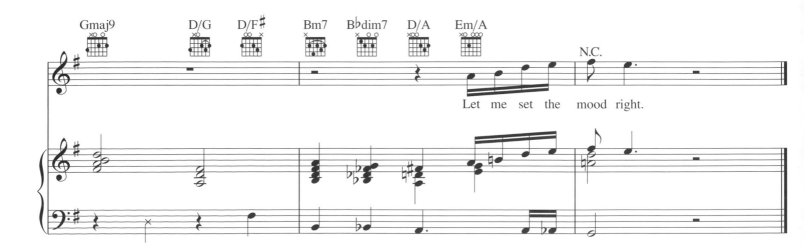

Let me set the mood right.

UNTIL THE END OF TIME

Words and Music by JUSTIN TIMBERLAKE,
TIM MOSLEY and NATE HILLS

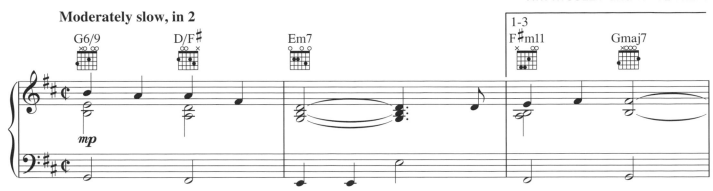

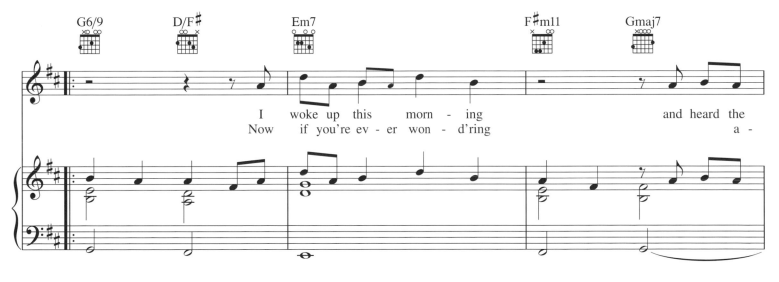

I woke up this morn - ing and heard the
Now if you're ev - er won - d'ring a -

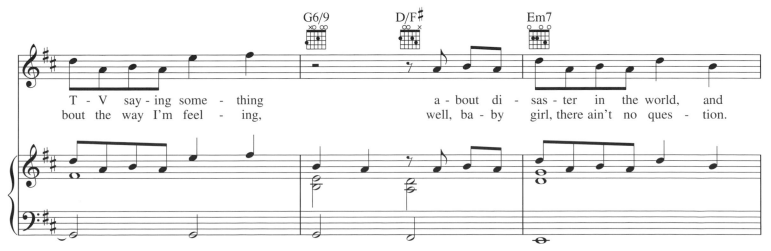

T - V say - ing some - thing a - bout di - sas - ter in the world, and
bout the way I'm feel - ing, well, ba - by girl, there ain't no ques - tion.

104

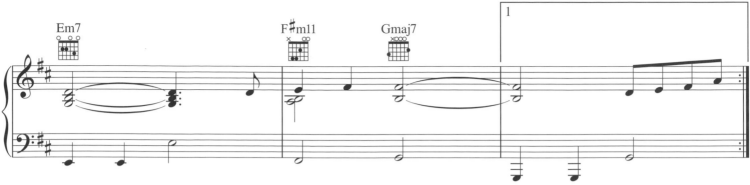

'Cause if your love was all I had

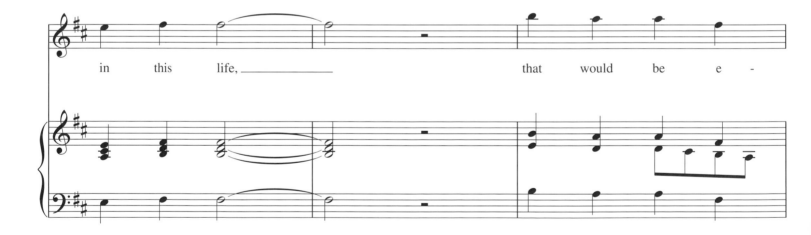

in this life, _____ that would be e -

nough un - til the end of time. _____

LOSING MY WAY

Words and Music by JUSTIN TIMBERLAKE,
TIM MOSLEY and NATE HILLS

Moderately, in 2

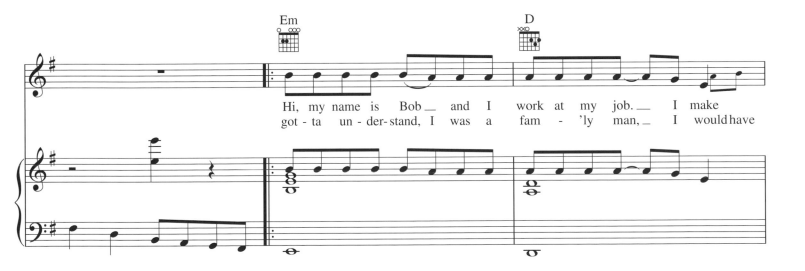

Hi, my name is Bob___ and I work at my job.___ I make
got-ta un-der-stand, I was a fam-'ly man,___ I would have

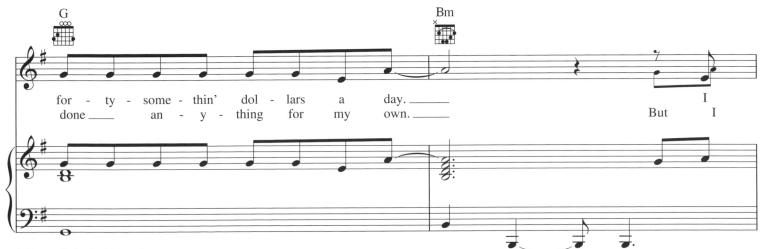

for-ty- some- thin' dol- lars a day.___
done ___ an-y-thing for my own.___ But I

I

* Recorded a half step lower.

can't put down the pipe.
col-or of my daugh-ter's eyes.
And it is break-ing me down.

Watch-ing the world spin 'round while my

dreams fall down. Is an-y-bod-y out there? It is

break-ing me down. No more friends a-round

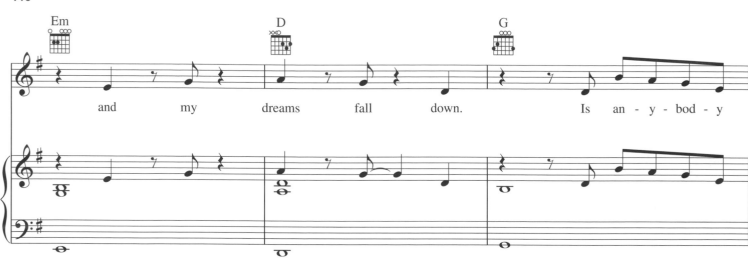

and my dreams fall down. Is an-y-bod-y

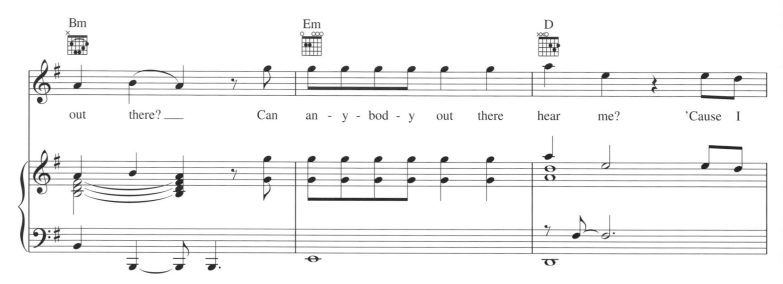

out there? ___ Can an-y-bod-y out there hear me? 'Cause I

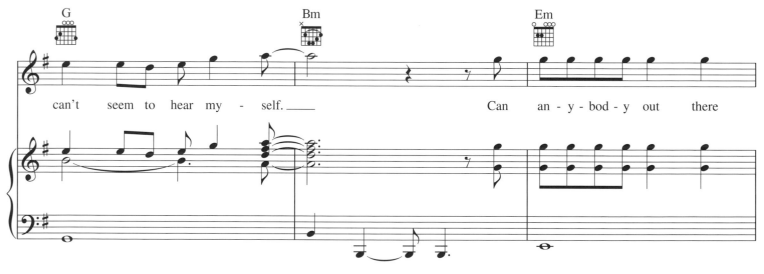

can't seem to hear my-self. ___ Can an-y-bod-y out there

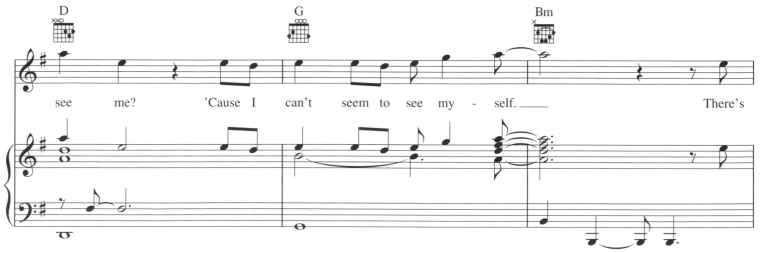

see me? 'Cause I can't seem to see my-self. ___ There's

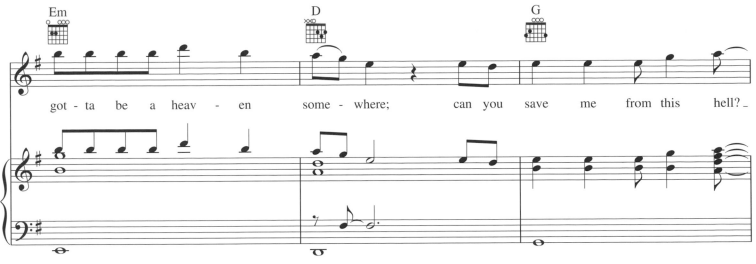

got-ta be a heav - en some - where; can you save me from this hell? _

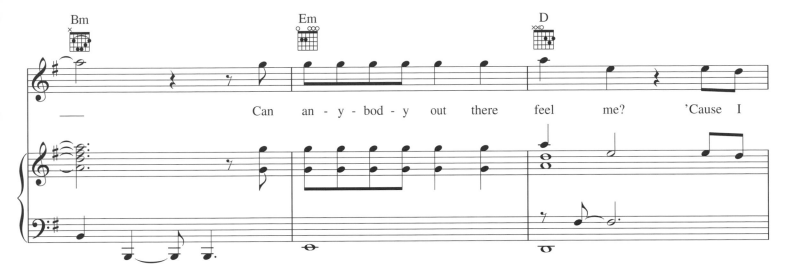

_ Can an - y - bod - y out there feel me? 'Cause I

can't seem to feel my - self. ____ Los - ing my way, ____

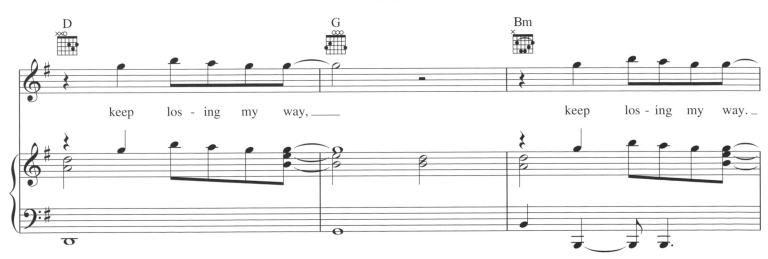

keep los - ing my way, ____ keep los - ing my way. _

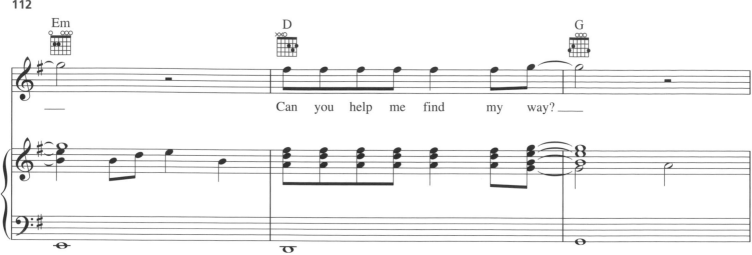

Can you help me find my way? ____

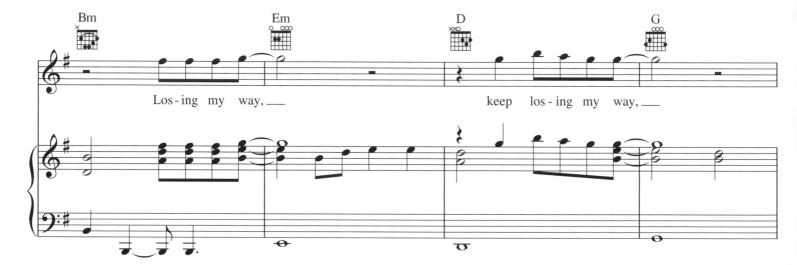

Los-ing my way, ____ keep los-ing my way, ____

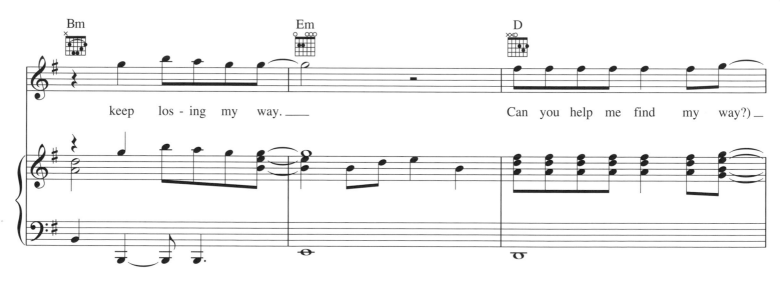

keep los-ing my way. ____ Can you help me find my way?) __

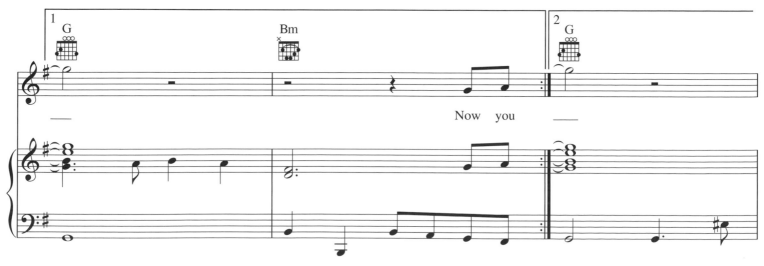

Now you ____

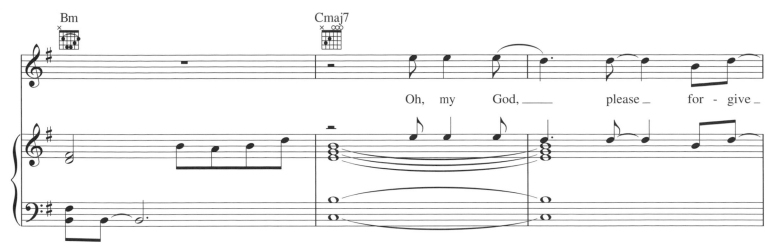

Oh, my God, _____ please _____ for-give _____

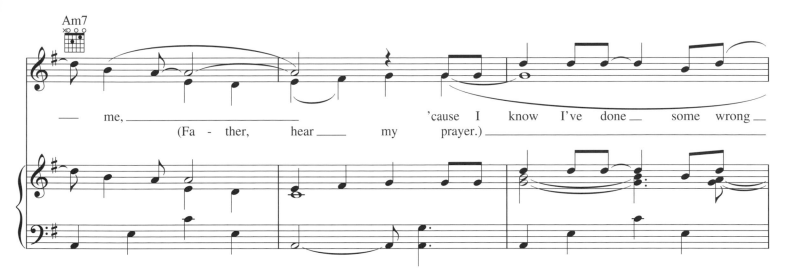

_____ me, _____ 'cause I know I've done _____ some wrong _____
(Fa - ther, hear _____ my prayer.) _____

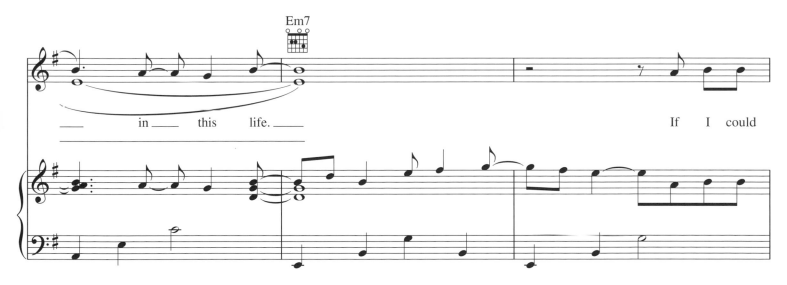

_____ in _____ this life. _____   If I could

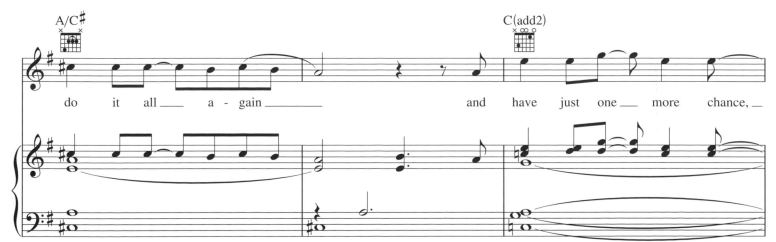

do it all _____ a - gain _____   and have just one _____ more chance, _____

take all ___ those wrongs ___ and make ___ them right.

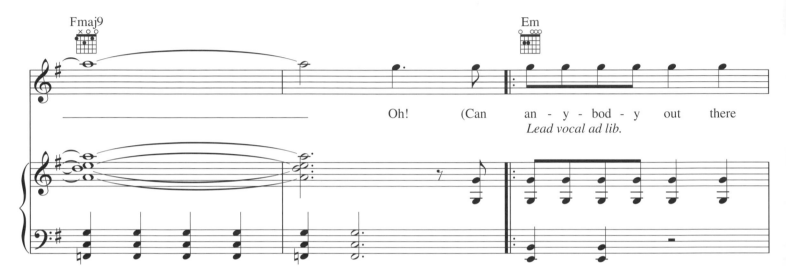

Oh!   (Can   an - y - bod - y   out   there
Lead vocal ad lib.

hear   me?   'Cause I   can't   seem to   hear my - self. ___   Can

an - y - bod - y   out   there   see   me?   'Cause I   can't   seem to   see my - self. ___

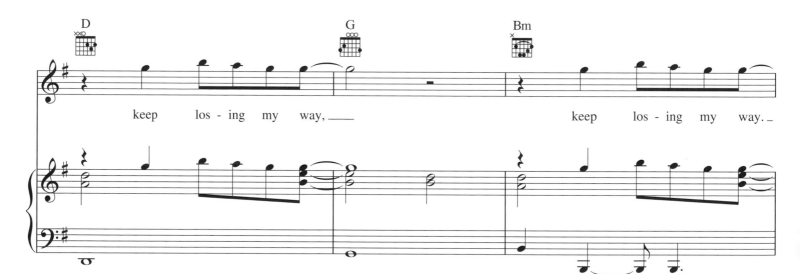

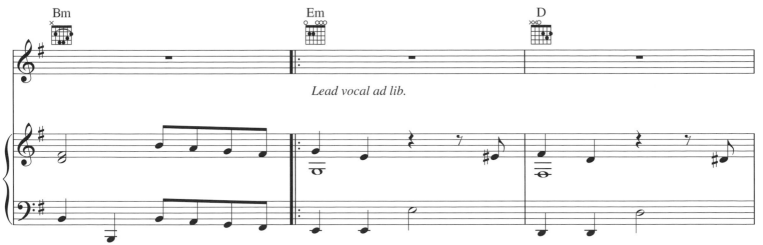

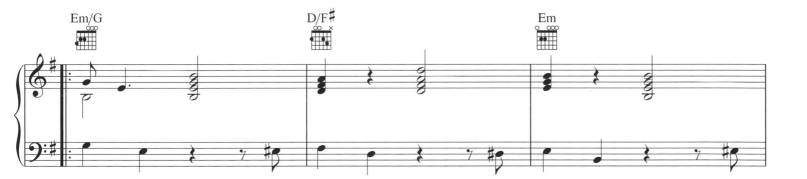

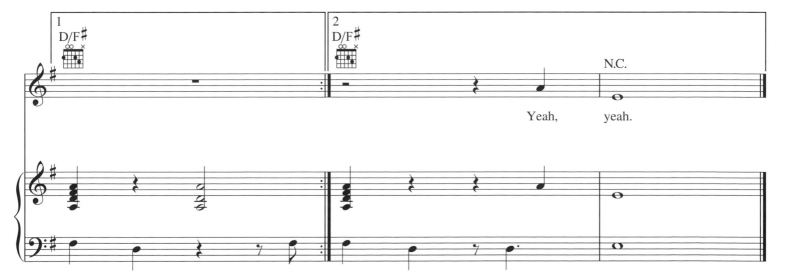

(Another Song)
ALL OVER AGAIN

Words and Music by JUSTIN TIMBERLAKE
and MATTHEW B. MORRIS

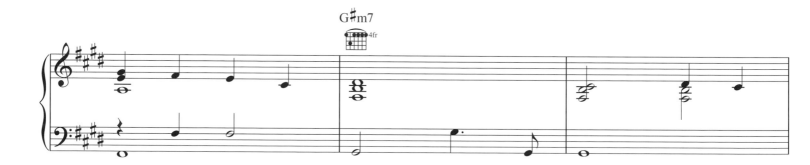

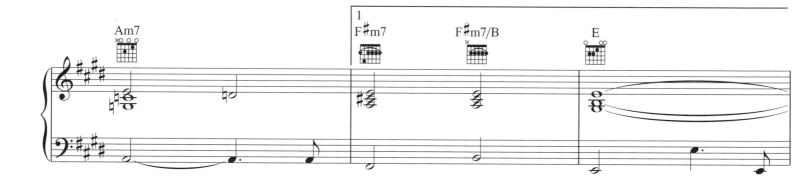

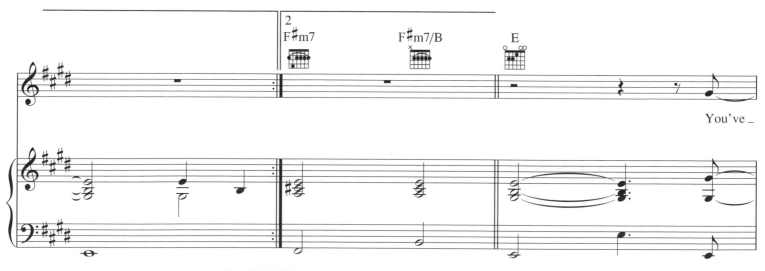

You've

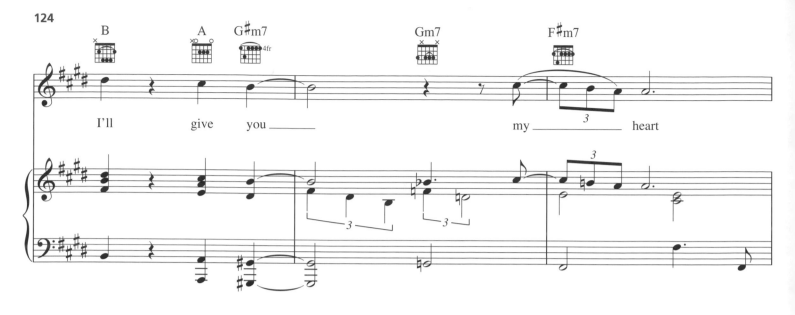

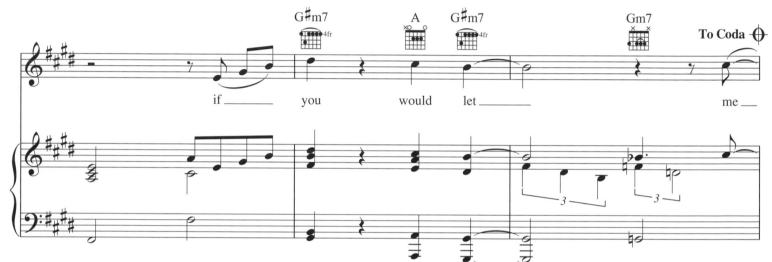

Lead vocal ad lib. to end

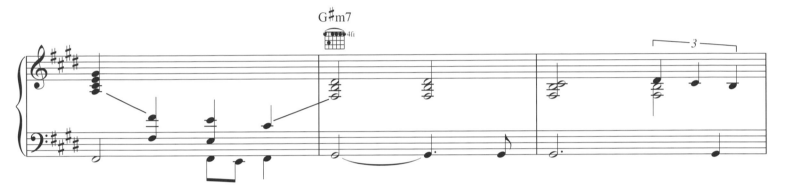

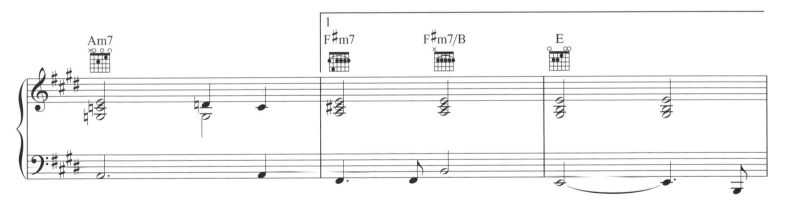